PROFIT AND LOSS

Profit and Loss

Ludwig von Mises

MISES
INSTITUTE
AUBURN, ALABAMA

Ludwig von Mises Institute
518 West Magnolia Avenue
Auburn, Ala. 36832
mises.org

ISBN: 978-1-61016-556-3

Contents

A. The Economic Nature of Profit and Loss

1. The Emergence of Profit and Loss

In the capitalist system of society's economic organization the entrepreneurs determine the course of production. In the performance of this function they are unconditionally and totally subject to the sovereignty of the buying public, the consumers. If they fail to produce in the cheapest and best possible way those commodities which the consumers are asking for most urgently, they suffer losses and are finally eliminated from their entrepreneurial position. Other men who know better how to serve the consumers replace them.

If all people were to anticipate correctly the future state of the market, the entrepreneurs would neither earn any profits nor suffer any losses. They would

Ludwig von Mises (1881–1973) was dean of the Austrian School of economics. This paper was prepared for the meeting of the Mont Pèlerin Society held in Beauvallon, France, September 9–16, 1951. It is included in *Planning for Freedom* (South Holland, Ill.: Libertarian Press, 1952).

have to buy the complementary factors of production at prices which would, already at the instant of the purchase, fully reflect the future prices of the products. No room would be left either for profit or for loss. What makes profit emerge is the fact that the entrepreneur who judges the future prices of the products more correctly than other people do buys some or all of the factors of production at prices which, seen from the point of view of the future state of the market, are too low. Thus the total costs of production—including interest on the capital invested—lag behind the prices which the entrepreneur receives for the product. This difference is entrepreneurial profit.

On the other hand, the entrepreneur who misjudges the future prices of the products allows for the factors of production prices which, seen from the point of view of the future state of the market, are too high. His total cost of production exceeds the prices at which he can sell the product. This difference is entrepreneurial loss.

Thus profit and loss are generated by success or failure in adjusting the course of production activities to the most urgent demand of the consumers. Once this adjustment is achieved, they disappear. The prices of the complementary factors of production reach a height at which total costs of production coincide with the price of the product. Profit and loss are ever-present features only on account of the fact that ceaseless change in the economic data makes again and again new discrepancies, and consequently the need for new adjustments originates.

2. The Distinction Between Profits and Other Proceeds

Many errors concerning the nature of profit and loss were caused by the practice of applying the term profit to the totality of the residual proceeds of an entrepreneur.

Interest on the capital employed is not a component part of profit. The dividends of a corporation are not profit. They are interest on the capital invested plus profit or minus loss.

The market equivalent of work performed by the entrepreneur in the conduct of the enterprise's affairs is entrepreneurial quasi-wages but not profit.

If the enterprise owns a factor on which it can earn monopoly prices, it makes a monopoly gain. If this enterprise is a corporation, such gains increase the dividend. Yet they are not profit proper.

Still more serious are the errors due to the confusion of entrepreneurial activity and technological innovation and improvement.

The maladjustment the removal of which is the essential function of entrepreneurship may often consist in the fact that new technological methods have not yet been utilized to the full extent to which they should be in order to bring about the best possible satisfaction of consumers' demand. But this is not necessarily always the case. Changes in the data, especially in consumers' demand, may require adjustments which have no reference at all to technological innovations and improvements. The entrepreneur who simply increases the production of an article by adding to the existing production facilities a new outfit without any change in the technological method of production is no less an entrepreneur than the man who inaugurates a new way of producing. The business of the entrepreneur is not merely to experiment with new technological methods, but to select from the multitude of technologically feasible methods those which are best fit to supply the public in the cheapest way with the things they are asking for most urgently. Whether a new technological procedure is or is not fit for this purpose is to be provisionally decided by the entrepreneur and will be finally decided by the conduct of the buying public. The question is not whether a new method is to be considered as a more "elegant" solution of a technological problem. It is whether, under the given state of economic data, it is the best possible method of supplying the consumers in the cheapest way.

The activities of the entrepreneur consist in making decisions. He determines for what purpose the factors of production should be employed. Any other acts which an entrepreneur may perform are merely accidental to his entrepreneurial function. It is this that laymen often fail to realize. They confuse the entrepreneurial activities with the conduct of the technological and administrative affairs of a plant. In their eyes not the stockholders, the promoters and speculators, but hired employees are the real entrepreneurs. The former are merely idle parasites who pocket the dividends.

Now nobody ever contended that one could produce without working. But neither is it possible to produce without capital goods, the previously produced factors of further production. These capital goods are scarce, i.e., they do not suffice for the production of all things which one would like to have produced. Hence the economic problem arises: to employ them in such a way that only those goods should be produced which are fit to satisfy the most urgent demands of the consumers. No good should remain unproduced on account of the fact that the factors required for its production were used—wasted—for the production of another good for which the demand of the public is less intense. To achieve this is under capitalism the function of entrepreneurship that determines the allocation of capital to the various branches of production. Under socialism it would be a function of the state, the social apparatus of coercion and oppression. The problem of whether a socialist directorate, lacking any method of economic calculation, could fulfill this function is not to be dealt with in this essay.

There is a simple rule of thumb to tell entrepreneurs from non-entrepreneurs. The entrepreneurs are those on whom the incidence of losses on the capital employed falls. Amateur-economists may confuse profits with other kinds of intakes. But it is impossible to fail to recognize losses on the capital employed.

3. Non-Profit Conduct of Affairs

What has been called the democracy of the market manifests itself in the fact that profit-seeking business is unconditionally subject to the supremacy of the buying public.

Non-profit organizations are sovereign unto themselves. They are, within the limits drawn by the amount of capital at their disposal, in a position to defy the wishes of the public.

A special case is that of the conduct of government affairs, the administration of the social apparatus of coercion and oppression, viz. the police power. The objectives of government, the protection of the inviolability of the individuals' lives and health and of their efforts to improve the material conditions of their existence, are indispensable. They benefit all and are the necessary prerequisite of social cooperation and civilization. But they cannot be sold and bought in the way merchandise is sold and bought; they have therefore no price on the market. With regard to them there cannot be any economic calculation. The costs expended for their conduct cannot be confronted with a price received for the product. This state of affairs would make the officers entrusted with the administration of governmental activities irresponsible despots if they were not curbed by the budget system. Under this system the administrators are forced to comply with detailed instructions enjoined upon them by the sovereign, be it a self-appointed autocrat or the whole people acting through elected representatives. To the officers limited funds are assigned which they are bound to spend only for those purposes which the sovereign has ordered. Thus the management of public administration becomes bureaucratic, i.e., dependent on definite detailed rules and regulations.

Bureaucratic management is the only alternative available where there is no profit and loss management.[1]

---

[1]Cf. Ludwig von Mises, Human Action: A Treatise on Economics (New Haven, Conn.: Yale University Press, 1949), pp. 306–07; *Bureaucracy*, (New Haven, Conn.: Yale University Press, 1944), pp. 40–73.

4. The Ballot of the Market

The consumers by their buying and abstention from buying elect the entrepreneurs in a daily repeated plebiscite as it were. They determine who should own and who not, and how much each owner should own.

As is the case with all acts of choosing a person— choosing holders of public office, employees, friends, or a consort—the decisions of the consumers are made on the ground of experience and thus necessarily always refers to the past. There is no experience of the future. The ballot of the market elevates those who in the immediate past have best served the consumers. However, the choice is not unalterable and can daily be corrected. The elected who disappoints the electorate is speedily reduced to the ranks.

Each ballot of the consumers adds only a little to the elected man's sphere of action. To reach the upper levels of entrepreneurship he needs a great number of votes, repeated again and again over a long period of time, a protracted series of successful strokes. He must stand every day a new trial, must submit anew to reelection as it were.

It is the same with his heirs. They can retain their eminent position only by receiving again and again confirmation on the part of the public. Their office is revocable. If they retain it, it is not on account of the deserts of their predecessor, but on account of their own ability to employ the capital for the best possible satisfaction of the consumers.

The entrepreneurs are neither perfect nor good in any metaphysical sense. They owe their position exclusively to the fact that they are better fit for the performance of the functions incumbent upon them than other people are. They earn profit not because they are clever in performing their tasks, but because they are more clever or less clumsy than other people are. They are not infallible and often blunder. But they are less liable to error and blunder less than other people do. Nobody has the right to take offense at the errors made by the entrepreneurs in the conduct of affairs and to stress the point that people would have been better supplied if the entrepreneurs had been more skillful and prescient. If the grumbler knew better, why did he not himself fill the gap and seize the opportunity to earn profits? It is easy indeed to display foresight after the event. In retrospect all fools become wise.

A popular chain of reasoning runs this way: The entrepreneur earns profit not only on account of the fact that other people were less successful than he in anticipating correctly the future state of the market. He himself contributed to the emergence of profit by not producing more of the article concerned; but for intentional restriction of output on his part, the supply of this article would have been so ample that the price would have dropped to a point at which no surplus of proceeds over costs of production expended would have emerged. This reasoning is at the bottom of the spurious doctrines of imperfect and monopolistic competition. It was resorted to a short time ago by the American Administration when it blamed the enterprises of the steel industry for the fact that the steel production capacity of the United States was not greater than it really was.

Certainly those engaged in the production of steel are not responsible for the fact that other people did not likewise enter this field of production. The reproach on the part of the authorities would have been sensible if they had conferred on the existing steel corporations the monopoly of steel production. But in the absence of such a privilege, the reprimand given to the operating mills is not more justified than it would be to censure the nation's poets and musicians for the fact that there are not more and better poets and musicians. If somebody is to blame for the fact that the number of people who joined the voluntary civilian defense organization is not larger, then it is not those who have already joined but only those who have not.

That the production of a commodity p is not larger than it really is, is due to the fact that the complementary factors of production required for an expansion were employed for the production of other commodities. To speak of an insufficiency of the supply of p is empty rhetoric if it does not indicate the various products m which were produced in too large quantities with the effect that their production appears now, i.e., after the event, as a waste of scarce factors of production. We may assume that the entrepreneurs who instead of producing additional quantities of p turned to the production of excessive amounts of m and consequently suffered losses, did not intentionally make their mistake.

Neither did the producers of p intentionally restrict the production of p. Every entrepreneur's capital is limited; he employs it for those projects which, he expects, will, by filling the most urgent demand of the public, yield the highest profit.

An entrepreneur at whose disposal are 100 units of capital employs, for instance, 50 units for the production of p and 50 units for the production of q. If both lines are profitable, it is odd to blame him for not having employed more, e.g., 75 units, for the production of p. He could increase the production of p only by curtailing correspondingly the production of q. But with regard to q the same fault could be found by the grumblers. If one blames the entrepreneur for not having produced more p, one must blame him also for not having produced more q. This means: one blames the entrepreneur for the facts that there is a scarcity of the factors of production and that the earth is not a land of Cockaigne.

Perhaps the grumbler will object on the ground that he considers p a vital commodity, much more important than q, and that therefore the production of p should be expanded and that of q restricted. If this is really the meaning of his criticism, he is at variance with the valuations of the consumers. He throws off his mask and shows his dictatorial aspirations. Production should not be directed by the wishes of the public but by his own despotic discretion.

But if our entrepreneur's production of q involves a loss, it is obvious that his fault was poor foresight and not intentional.

Entrance into the ranks of the entrepreneurs in a market society, not sabotaged by the interference of government or other agencies resorting to violence, is open to everybody. Those who know how to take advantage of any business opportunity cropping up will always find the capital required. For the market is always full of capitalists anxious to find the most promising employment for their funds and in search of the ingenious newcomers, in partnership with whom they could execute the most remunerative projects.

People often failed to realize this inherent feature of capitalism because they did not grasp the meaning and the effects of capital scarcity. The task of the entrepreneur is to select from the multitude of technologically feasible projects those which will satisfy the most urgent of the not yet satisfied needs of the public. Those projects for the execution of which the capital supply does not suffice must not be carried out. The market is always crammed with visionaries who want to float such impracticable and unworkable schemes. It is these dreamers who always complain about the blindness of the capitalists who are too stupid to look after their own interests. Of course, the investors often err in the choice of their investments. But these faults consist precisely in the fact that they preferred an unsuitable project to another that would have satisfied more urgent needs of the buying public.

People often err very lamentably in estimating the work of the creative genius. Only a minority of men are appreciative enough to attach the right value to the achievement of poets, artists, and thinkers. It may happen that the indifference of his contemporaries makes it impossible for a genius to accomplish what he would have accomplished if his fellow men had displayed better judgment. The way in which the poet laureate and the philosopher *à la mode* are selected is certainly questionable.

But it is impermissible to question the free market's choice of the entrepreneurs. The consumers' preference for definite articles may be open to condemnation from the point of view of a philosopher's judgment. But judgments of value are necessarily always personal and subjective. The consumer chooses what, as he thinks, satisfies him best. Nobody is called upon to determine what could make another man happier or less unhappy. The popularity of motor cars, television sets, and nylon stockings may be criticized from a "higher" point of view. But these are the things that people are asking for. They cast their ballots for those entrepreneurs who offer them this merchandise of the best quality at the cheapest price.

In choosing between various political parties and programs for the commonwealth's social and economic organization most people are uninformed and groping in the dark. The average voter lacks the insight to distinguish between policies suitable to attain the ends he is aiming at and those unsuitable. He is at a loss to examine the long chains of aprioristic reasoning which constitute the philosophy of a comprehensive social program. He may at best form some opinion about the short-run effects of the policies concerned. He is helpless in dealing with the long-run effects. The socialists and communists in principle often assert the infallibility of majority decisions. However, they belie their own words in criticizing parliamentary majorities rejecting their creed, and in denying to the people, under the one-party system, the opportunity to choose between different parties.

But in buying a commodity or abstaining from its purchase there is nothing else involved than the consumer's longing for the best possible satisfaction of his instantaneous wishes. The consumer does not—like the voter in political voting—choose between different means whose effects appear only later. He chooses between things which immediately provide satisfaction. His decision is final.

An entrepreneur earns profit by serving the consumers, the people, as they are and not as they should be according to the fancies of some grumbler or potential dictator.

5. The Social Function of Profit and Loss

Profits are never normal. They appear only where there is a maladjustment, a divergence between actual production and production as it should be in order to utilize the available material and mental resources for the best possible satisfaction of the wishes of the public. They are the prize of those who remove this maladjustment; they disappear as soon as the maladjustment is entirely removed. In the imaginary construction of an evenly rotating economy there are no profits. There the sum of the prices of the complementary factors of production, due allowance being made for time preference, coincides with the price of the product.

The greater the preceding maladjustments, the greater the profit earned by their removal. Maladjustments may sometimes be called excessive. But it is inappropriate to apply the epithet "excessive" to profits.

People arrive at the idea of excessive profits by confronting the profit earned with the capital employed in the enterprise and measuring the profit as a percentage of the capital. This method is suggested by the customary procedure applied in partnerships and corporations for the assignment of quotas of the total profit to the individual partners and shareholders. These men have contributed to a different extent to the realization of the project and share in the profits and losses according to the extent of their contribution.

But it is not the capital employed that creates profits and losses. Capital does not "beget profit" as Marx thought. The capital goods as such are dead things that in themselves do not accomplish anything. If they are utilized according to a good idea, profit results. If they are utilized according to a mistaken idea, no profit or losses result. It is the entrepreneurial decision that creates either profit or loss. It is mental acts, the mind of the entrepreneur, from which profits ultimately originate. Profit is a product of the mind, of success in anticipating the future state of the market. It is a spiritual and intellectual phenomenon.

The absurdity of condemning any profits as excessive can easily be shown. An enterprise with a capital of the amount c produced a definite quantity of p which it sold at prices that brought a surplus of proceeds over costs of s and consequently a profit of n per cent. If the entrepreneur had been less capable, he would have needed a capital of $2c$ for the production of the same quantity of p. For the sake of argument we may even neglect the fact that this would have necessarily increased costs of production as it would have doubled the interest on the capital employed, and we may assume that s would have remained unchanged. But at any rate s would have been confronted with $2c$ instead of c and thus the profit would have been only $n/2$ per cent of the capital employed. The "excessive" profit would have been reduced to a "fair" level. Why? Because the entrepreneur was less efficient and because his lack of efficiency deprived his fellow men of all the advantages they could have got if an amount c of capital goods had been left available for the production of other merchandise.

In branding profits as excessive and penalizing the efficient entrepreneurs by discriminatory taxation, people are injuring themselves. Taxing profits is tantamount to taxing success in best serving the public. The only goal of all production activities is to employ the factors of production in such a way that they render the highest possible output. The smaller the input required for the production of an article becomes, the more of the scarce factors of production are left for the production of other articles. But the better an entrepreneur succeeds in this regard, the more is he vilified and the more is he soaked by taxation. Increasing costs per unit of output, that is, waste, is praised as a virtue.

The most amazing manifestation of this complete failure to grasp the task of production and the nature and functions of profit and loss is shown in the popular superstition that profit is an addendum to the costs of production, the height of which depends uniquely on the discretion of the seller. It is this belief that guides governments in controlling prices. It is the same belief that has prompted many governments to make arrangements with their contractors according to which the price to be paid for an article delivered is to equal costs of production expended by the seller increased by a definite percentage. The effect was that the purveyor got a surplus the higher, the less he succeeded in avoiding superfluous costs. Contracts of this type enhanced considerably the sums the United States had to expend in the two World Wars. But the bureaucrats, first of all the professors of economics who served in the various war agencies, boasted of their clever handling of the matter.

All people, entrepreneurs as well as non-entrepreneurs, look askance upon any profits earned by other people. Envy is a common weakness of men. People are loath to acknowledge the fact that they themselves could have earned profits if they had displayed the same foresight and judgment the successful businessman did. Their resentment is the more violent, the more they are subconsciously aware of this fact.

There would not be any profits but for the eagerness of the public to acquire the merchandise offered for sale by the successful entrepreneur. But the same people who scramble for these articles vilify the businessman and call his profit ill-got.

The semantic expression of this enviousness is the distinction between earned and unearned income. It permeates the textbooks, the language of the laws and administrative procedure. Thus, for instance, the official Form 201 for the New York State Income Tax Return calls "Earnings" only the compensation received by employees and, by implication, all other income, also that resulting from the exercise of a profession, unearned income. Such is the terminology of a state whose governor is a Republican and whose state assembly has a Republican majority.

Public opinion condones profits only as far as they do not exceed the salary paid to an employee. All surplus is rejected as unfair. The objective of taxation is, under the ability-to-pay principle, to confiscate this surplus.

Now one of the main functions of profits is to shift the control of capital to those who know how to employ it in the best possible way for the satisfaction of the public. The more profits a man earns, the greater his wealth consequently becomes, the more influential does he become in the conduct of business affairs. Profit and loss are the instruments by means of which the consumers pass the direction of production activities into the hands of those who are best fit to serve them. Whatever is undertaken to curtail or to confiscate profits impairs this function. The result of such measures is to loosen the grip the consumers hold over the course of production. The economic machine becomes, from the point of view of the people, less efficient and less responsive.

The jealousy of the common man looks upon the profits of the entrepreneurs as if they were totally used for consumption. A part of them is, of course, consumed. But only those entrepreneurs attain wealth and influence in the realm of business who consume merely a fraction of their proceeds and plough back the much greater part into their enterprises. What makes small business develop into big business is not spending, but saving and capital accumulation.

6. Profit and Loss in the Progressing and in the Retrogressing Economy

We call a stationary economy an economy in which the per head quota of the income and wealth of the individuals remains unchanged. In such an economy what the consumers spend more for the purchase of some articles must be equal to what they spend less for other articles. The total amount of the profits earned by one part of the entrepreneurs equals the total amount of losses suffered by other entrepreneurs.

A surplus of the sum of all profits earned in the whole economy above the sum of all losses suffered emerges only in a progressing economy, that is in an economy in which the per head quota of capital increases. This increment is an effect of saving that adds new capital goods to the quantity already previously available. The increase of capital available creates maladjustments insofar as it brings about a discrepancy between the actual state of production and that state which the additional capital makes possible. Thanks to the emergence of additional capital, certain projects which hitherto could not be executed become feasible. In directing the new capital into those channels in which it satisfies the most urgent among the previously not satisfied wants of the consumers, the entrepreneurs earn profits which are not counterbalanced by the losses of other entrepreneurs.

The enrichment which the additional capital generates goes only in part to those who have created it by saving. The rest goes, by raising the marginal productivity of labor and thereby wage rates, to the earners of wages and salaries and, by raising the prices of definite raw materials and food stuffs, to the owners of land, and, finally, to the entrepreneurs who integrate this new capital into the most economical production processes. But while the gain of the wage earners and of the landowners is permanent, the profits of the entrepreneurs disappear once this integration is accomplished. Profits of the entrepreneurs are, as has been mentioned already, a permanent phenomenon only on account of the fact that maladjustments appear daily anew by the elimination of which profits are earned.

Let us for the sake of argument resort to the concept of national income as employed in popular economics. Then it is obvious that in a stationary economy no part of the national income goes into profits. Only in a progressing economy is there a surplus of total profits over total losses. The popular belief that profits are a deduction from the income of workers and consumers is entirely fallacious. If we want to apply the term deduction to the issue, we have to say that this surplus of profits over losses as well as the increments of the wage earners and the landowners is deducted from the gains of those whose saving brought about the additional capital. It is their saving that is the vehicle of economic improvment, that makes the employment of technological innovations possible and raises productivity and the standard of living. It is the entrepreneurs whose activity takes care of the most economical employment of the additional capital. As far as they themselves do not save, neither the workers nor the landowners contribute anything to the emergence of the circumstances which generate what is called economic progress and improvement. They are benefited by other peoples' saving that creates additional capital on the one hand and by the entrepreneurial action that directs this additional capital toward the satisfaction of the most urgent wants on the other hand. A retrogressing economy is an economy in which the per head quota of capital invested is decreasing. In such an economy the total amount of losses incurred by entrepreneurs exceeds the total amount of profits earned by other entrepreneurs.

7. The Computation of Profit and Loss

The originary praxeological categories of profit and loss are psychic qualities and not reducible to any interpersonal description in quantitative terms. They are intensive magnitudes. The difference between the value of the end attained and that of the means applied for its attainment is profit if it is positive and loss if it is negative.

Where there are social division of efforts and cooperation as well as private ownership of the means of production, economic calculation in terms of monetary units becomes feasible and necessary. Profit and loss are computable as social phenomena. The psychic phenomena of profit and loss, from which they are ultimately derived, remain, of course, incalculable intensive magnitudes.

The fact that in the frame of the market economy entrepreneurial profit and loss are determined by arithmetical operations has misled many people. They fail to see that essential items that enter into this calculation are estimates emanating from the entrepreneur's specific understanding of the future state of the market. They think that these computations are open to examination and verification or alteration on the part of a disinterested expert. They ignore the fact that such computations are as a rule an inherent part of the entrepreneur's speculative anticipation of uncertain future conditions.

For the task of this essay it suffices to refer to one of the problems of cost accounting. One of the items of a bill of costs is the establishment of the difference between the price paid for the acquisition of what is commonly called durable production equipment and its present value. This present value is the money equivalent of the contribution this equipment will make to future earnings. There is no certainty about the future state of the market and about the height of these earnings. They can only be determined by a speculative anticipation on the part of the entrepreneur. It is preposterous to call in an expert and to substitute his arbitrary judgment for that of the entrepreneur. The expert is objective insofar as he is not affected by an error made. But the entrepreneur exposes his own material well-being.

Of course, the law determines magnitudes which it calls profit and loss. But these magnitudes are not identical with the economic concepts of profit and loss and must not be confused with them. If a tax law calls a magnitude profit, it in effect determines the height of taxes due. It calls this magnitude profit because it wants to justify its tax policy in the eyes of the public. It would be more correct for the legislator to omit the term profit and simply to speak of the basis for the computation of the tax due.

The tendency of the tax laws is to compute what they call profit as high as possible in order to increase immediate public revenue. But there are other laws which are committed to the tendency to restrict the magnitude they call profit. The commercial codes of many nations were and are guided by the endeavor to protect the rights of creditors. They aimed at restricting what they called profit in order to prevent the entrepreneur from withdrawing to the prejudice of creditors too much from the firm or corporation for his own benefit. It was these tendencies which were operative in the evolution of the commercial usages concerning the customary height of depreciation quotas.

There is no need today to dwell upon the problem of the falsification of economic calculation under inflationary conditions. All people begin to comprehend the phenomenon of illusory profits, the offshoot of the great inflations of our age.

Failure to grasp the effects of inflation upon the customary methods of computing profits originated the modern concept of *profiteering*. An entrepreneur is dubbed a profiteer if his profit and loss statement, calculated in terms of a currency subject to a rapidly progressing inflation, shows profits which other people deem "excessive." It has happened very often in many countries that the profit and loss statement of such a profiteer, when calculated in terms of a noninflated or less inflated currency, showed not only no profit at all but considerable losses.

Even if we neglect for the sake of argument any reference to the phenomenon of merely inflation-induced illusory profits, it is obvious that the epithet profiteer is the expression of an arbitrary judgment of value. There is no other standard available for the distinction between profiteering and earning fair profits than that provided by the censor's personal envy and resentment.

It is strange indeed that an eminent logician, the late L. Susan Stebbing, entirely failed to perceive the issue involved. Professor Stebbing equated the concept of profiteering to concepts which refer to a clear distinction of such a nature that no sharp line can be drawn between extremes. The distinction between excess profits or profiteering, and "legitimate profits," she declared, is clear, although it is not a sharp distinction.[2] Now this distinction is clear only in reference to an act of legislation that defines the term excess profits as used in its context. But this is not what Stebbing had in mind. She explicitly emphasized that such legal definitions are made "in an arbitrary manner for the practical purposes of administration." She used the term *legitimate* without any reference to legal statutes and their definitions. But is it permissible to employ the term legitimate without reference to any standard from the point of view of which the thing in question is to be considered as legitimate? And is there any other standard available for the distinction between profiteering and legitimate profits than one provided by personal judgments of value?

Professor Stebbing referred to the famous *acervus* and *calvus* arguments of the old logicians. Many words are vague insofar as they apply to characteristics which

---

[2]Cf. L. Susan Stebbing, *Thinking to Some Purpose* (New York: Pelican Books, 1939), pp. 185–87.

may be possessed in varying degrees. It is impossible to draw a sharp line between those who are bald and those who are not. It is impossible to define precisely the concept of baldness. But what Professor Stebbing failed to notice is that the characteristic according to which people distinguish between those who are bald and those who are not is open to a precise definition. It is the presence or the absence of hair on the head of a person. This is a clear and unambiguous mark of which the presence or absence is to be established by observation and to be expressed by propositions about existence. What is vague is merely the determination of the point at which non-baldness turns into baldness. People may disagree with regard to the determination of this point. But their disagreements refer to the interpretation of the convention that attaches a certain meaning to the word baldness. No judgments of value are implied. It may, of course, happen that the difference of opinion is in a concrete case caused by bias. But this is another thing.

The vagueness of words like bald is the same that is inherent in the indefinite numerals and pronouns. Language needs such terms, as for many purposes of daily communication between men, an exact arithmetical establishment of quantities is superfluous and too bothersome. Logicians are badly mistaken in attempting to attach to such words, whose vagueness is intentional and serves definite purposes, the precision of the definite numerals. For an individual who plans to visit Seattle the information that there are many hotels in this city is sufficient. A committee that plans to hold a convention in Seattle needs precise information about the number of hotel beds available.

Professor Stebbing's error consisted in the confusion of existential propositions with judgments of value. Her unfamiliarity with the problems of economics, which all her otherwise valuable writings display, led her astray. She would not have made such a blunder in a field that was better known to her. She would not have declared that there is a clear distinction between an author's "legitimate royalties" and "illegitimate royalties." She would have comprehended that the height of the royalties depends on the public's appreciation of a book and that an observer who criticizes the height of royalties merely expresses his personal judgment of value.

B. The Condemnation of Profit

1. Economics and the Abolition of Profit

Those who spurn entrepreneurial profit as "unearned" mean that it is lucre unfairly withheld either from the workers or from the consumers or from both. Such is the idea underlying the alleged "right to the whole produce of labor" and the Marxian doctrine of exploitation. It can be said that most governments—if not all—and the immense majority of our contemporaries by and large endorse this opinion although some of them are generous enough to acquiesce in the suggestion that a fraction of profits should be left to the "exploiters."

There is no use in arguing about the adequacy of ethical precepts. They are derived from intuition; they are arbitrary and subjective. There is no objective standard available with regard to which they could be judged. Ultimate ends are chosen by the individual's judgments of value. They cannot be determined by scientific inquiry and logical reasoning. If a man says, "This is what I am aiming at whatever the consequences of my conduct and the price I shall have to pay for it may be," nobody is in a position to oppose any arguments against him. But the question is whether it is really true that this man is ready to pay any price for the attainment of the end concerned. If this latter question is answered in the negative, it becomes possible to enter into an examination of the issue involved.

If there were really people who are prepared to put up with all the consequences of the abolition of profit, however detrimental they may be, it would not be possible for economics to deal with the problem. But this is not the case. Those who want to abolish profit are guided by the idea that this confiscation would improve the material well-being of all non-entrepreneurs. In their eyes the abolition of profit is not an ultimate end but a means for the attainment of a definite end, viz., the enrichment of the non-entrepreneurs. Whether this end can really be attained by the employment of this means and whether the employment of this means does not perhaps bring about some other effects which may to some or to all people appear more undesirable than conditions before the employment of this means, these are questions which economics is called upon to examine.

2. The Consequences of the Abolition of Profit

The idea to abolish profit for the advantage of the consumers involves that the entrepreneur should be forced to sell the products at prices not exceeding the costs of production expended. As such prices are, for all articles the sale of which would have brought profit, below the potential market price, the available supply is not sufficient to make it possible for all those who want to buy at these prices to acquire the articles. The market is paralyzed by the maximum price decree. It can no longer allocate the products to the consumers. A system of rationing must be adopted.

The suggestion to abolish the entrepreneur's profit for the benefit of the employees aims not at the abolition of profit. It aims at wresting it from the hands of the entrepreneur and handing it over to his employees.

Under such a scheme the incidence of losses incurred falls upon the entrepreneur, while profits go to the employees. It is probable that the effect of this arrangement would consist in making losses increase and profits dwindle. At any rate, a greater part of the profits would be consumed and less would be saved and ploughed back into the enterprise. No capital would be available for the establishment of new branches of production and for the transfer of capital from branches which—in compliance with the demand of the customers—should shrink into branches which should expand. For it would harm the interests of those employed in a definite enterprise or branch to restrict the capital employed in it and to transfer it into another enterprise or branch. If such a scheme had been adopted half a century ago, all the innovations accomplished in this period would have been rendered impossible. If, for the sake of argument, we were prepared to neglect any reference to the problem of capital accumulation, we would still have to realize that giving profit to the employees must result in rigidity of the once attained state of production and preclude any adjustment, improvement, and progress.

In fact, the scheme would transfer ownership of the capital invested into the hands of the employees. It would be tantamount to the establishment of syndicalism and would generate all the effects of syndicalism, a system which no author or reformer ever had the courage to advocate openly.

A third solution of the problem would be to confiscate all the profits earned by the entrepreneurs for the benefit of the state. A one hundred per cent tax on profits would accomplish this task. It would transform the entrepreneurs into irresponsible administrators of all plants and workshops. They would no longer be subject to the supremacy of the buying public. They would just be people who have the power to deal with production as it pleases them.

The policies of all contemporary governments which have not adopted outright socialism apply all these three schemes jointly. They confiscate by various measures of price control a part of the potential profits for the alleged benefit of the consumers. They support the labor unions in their endeavors to wrest, under the ability-to-pay principle of wage determination, a part of the profits from the entrepreneurs. And, last but not least, they are intent upon confiscating, by progressive income taxes, special taxes on corporation income and "excess profits" taxes, an ever increasing part of profits for public revenue. It can easily be seen that these policies if continued will very soon succeed in abolishing entrepreneurial profit altogether.

The joint effect of the application of these policies is already today rising chaos. The final effect will be the full realization of socialism by smoking out the entrepreneurs. Capitalism cannot survive the abolition of profit. It is profit and loss that force the capitalists to employ their capital for the best possible service to the consumers. It is profit and loss that make those people supreme in the conduct of business who are best fit to satisfy the public. If profit is abolished, chaos results.

3. The Anti-Profit Arguments

All the reasons advanced in favor of an anti-profit policy are the outcome of an erroneous interpretation of the operation of the market economy.

The tycoons are too powerful, too rich, and too big. They abuse their power for their own enrichment. They are irresponsible tyrants. Bigness of an enterprise is in itself an evil. There is no reason why some men should own millions while others are poor. The wealth of the few is the cause of the poverty of the masses.

Each word of these passionate denunciations is false. The businessmen are not irresponsible tyrants. It is precisely the necessity of making profits and avoiding losses that gives to the consumers a firm hold over the entrepreneurs and forces them to comply with the wishes of the people. What makes a firm big is its success in best filling the demands of the buyers. If the bigger enterprise did not better serve the people than a smaller one, it would long since have been reduced to smallness. There is no harm in a businessman's endeavors to enrich himself by increasing his profits. The businessman has in his capacity as a businessman only one task: to strive after the highest possible profit. Huge profits are the proof of good service rendered in supplying the consumers. Losses are the proof of blunders committed, of failure to perform satisfactorily the tasks incumbent upon an entrepreneur. The riches of successful entrepreneurs are not the cause of anybody's poverty; it is the consequence of the fact that the consumers are better supplied than they would have been in the absence of the entrepreneur's effort. The penury of millions in the backward countries is not caused by anybody's opulence; it is the correlative of the fact that their country lacks entrepreneurs who have acquired riches. The standard of living of the common man is highest in those countries which have the greatest number of wealthy entrepreneurs. It is to the foremost material interest of everybody that control of the factors of production should be concentrated in the hands of those who know how to utilize them in the most efficient way.

It is the avowed objective of the policies of all present-day governments and political parties to prevent the emergence of new millionaires. If this policy had been adopted in the United States fifty years ago the growth of the industries producing new articles would have been stunted. Motorcars, refrigerators, radio sets, and a hundred other less spectacular but even more useful innovations would not have become standard equipment in most of the American family households.

The average wage earner thinks that nothing else is needed to keep the social apparatus of production running and to improve and to increase output than the comparatively simple routine work assigned to him. He does not realize that the mere toil and trouble of the routinist is not sufficient. Sedulousness and skill are spent in vain if they are not directed toward the most important goal by the entrepreneur's foresight and are not aided by the capital accumulated by capitalists. The American worker is badly mistaken when he believes that his high standard of living is due to his own excellence. He is neither more industrious nor more skillful than the workers of Western Europe. He owes his superior income to the fact that his country clung to "rugged individualism" much longer than Europe. It was his luck that the United States turned to an anticapitalistic policy as much as forty or fifty years later than Germany. His wages are higher than those of the workers of the rest of the world because the capital equipment per head of the employee is highest in America and because the American entrepreneur was not so much restricted by crippling regimentation as his colleagues in other areas. The comparatively greater prosperity of the United States is an outcome of the fact that the New Deal did not come in 1900 or 1910, but only in 1933.

If one wants to study the reasons for Europe's backwardness, it would be necessary to examine the manifold laws and regulations that prevented in Europe the establishment of an equivalent of the American drug store and crippled the evolution of chain stores, department stores, super markets, and kindred outfits. It would be important to investigate the German Reich's effort to protect the inefficient methods of traditional *Handwerk* (handicraft) against the competition of capitalist business. Still more revealing would be an examination of the Austrian *Gewerbepolitik*, a policy that from the early eighties on aimed at preserving the economic structure of the ages preceding the Industrial Revolution.

The worst menace to prosperity and civilization and to the material well-being of the wage earners is the inability of union bosses, of "union economists" and of the less intelligent strata of the workers themselves to appreciate the role entrepreneurs play in production. This lack of insight has found a classical expression in the writings of Lenin. As Lenin saw it all that production requires besides the manual work of the laborer and the designing of the engineers is "control of production and distribution," a task that can easily be accomplished "by the armed workers." For this accounting and control "have been *simplified* by capitalism to the utmost, till they have become the extraordinarily simple operations of watching, recording and issuing receipts, within the reach of everybody who can read and write and knows the first four rules of arithmetic."[3] No further comment is needed.

4. The Equality Argument

In the eyes of the parties who style themselves progressive and leftist the main vice of capitalism is the inequality of incomes and wealth. The ultimate end of their policies is to establish equality. The moderates want to attain this goal step by step; the radicals plan to attain it at one stroke, by a revolutionary overthrow of the capitalist mode of production.

---

[3]V.I. Lenin, *State and Revolution* (New York: Edition by International Publishers, 1917), pp. 83–84). The italics are Lenin's (or the communist translator's).

However, in talking about equality and asking vehemently for its realization, nobody advocates a curtailment of his own present income. The term equality as employed in contemporary political language always means upward leveling of one's income, never downward leveling. It means getting more, not sharing one's own affluence with people who have less.

If the American automobile worker, railroadman, or compositor says equality, he means expropriating the holders of shares and bonds for his own benefit. He does not consider sharing with the unskilled workers who earn less. At best, he thinks of equality of all American citizens. It never occurs to him that the peoples of Latin America, Asia, and Africa may interpret the postulate of equality as world equality and not as national equality.

The political labor movement as well as the labor union movement flamboyantly advertise their internationalism. But this internationalism is a mere rhetorical gesture without any substantial meaning. In every country in which average wage rates are higher than in any other area, the unions advocate insurmountable immigration barriers in order to prevent foreign "comrades" and "brothers" from competing with their own members. Compared with the anti-immigration laws of the European nations, the immigration legislation of the American republics is mild indeed because it permits the immigration of a limited number of people. No such normal quotas are provided in most of the European laws.

All the arguments advanced in favor of income equalization within a country can with the same justification or lack of justification also be advanced in favor of world equalization. An American worker has

no better title to claim the savings of the American capitalist than has any foreigner. That a man has earned
profits by serving the consumers and has not entirely
consumed his funds but ploughed back the greater
part of them into industrial equipment does not give
anybody a valid title to expropriate this capital for his
own benefit. But if one maintains the opinion to the
contrary, there is certainly no reason to ascribe to anybody a better right to expropriate than to anybody
else. There is no reason to assert that only Americans
have the right to expropriate other Americans. The big
shots of American business are the scions of people
who immigrated to the United States from England,
Scotland, Ireland, France, Germany, and other European countries. The people of their country of origin
contend that they have the same title to seize the prop-
erty acquired by these men as the American people
have. The American radicals are badly mistaken in
believing that their social program is identical or at least
compatible with the objectives of the radicals of other
countries. It is not. The foreign radicals will not acquiesce in leaving to the Americans, a minority of less than
7 percent of the world's total population, what they
think is a privileged position. A world government of
the kind the American radicals are asking for would try
to confiscate by a world income tax all the surplus an
average American earns above the average income of a
Chinese or Indian worker. Those who question the cor-
rectness of this statement, would drop their doubts after
a conversation with any of the intellectual leaders of
Asia.

There is hardly any Iranian who would qualify the
objections raised by the British Labour Government
against the confiscation of the oil wells as anything

else but a manifestation of the most reactionary spirit of capitalist exploitation. Today governments abstain from virtually expropriating—by foreign exchange control, discriminatory taxation and similar devices— foreign investments only if they expect to get in the next years more foreign capital and thus to be able in the future to expropriate a greater amount.

The disintegration of the international capital market is one of the most important effects of the anti-profit mentality of our age. But no less disastrous is the fact that the greater part of the world's population looks upon the United States—not only upon the American capitalists but also upon the American workers—with the same feelings of envy, hatred, and hostility with which, stimulated by the socialist and communist doctrines, the masses everywhere look upon the capitalists of their own nation.

5. Communism and Poverty

A customary method of dealing with political programs and movements is to explain and to justify their popularity by referring to the conditions which people found unsatisfactory and to the goals they wanted to attain by the realization of these programs.

However, the only thing that matters is whether or not the program concerned is fit to attain the ends sought. A bad program and a bad policy can never be explained, still less justified by pointing to the unsatisfactory conditions of its originators and supporters. The sole question that counts is whether or not these policies can remove or alleviate the evils which they are designed to remedy.

Yet almost all our contemporaries declare again and again: If you want to succeed in fighting communism, socialism, and interventionism, you must first of all improve peoples' material conditions. The policy of *laissez faire* aims precisely at making people more prosperous. But it cannot succeed as long as want is worsened more and more by socialist and interventionist measures.

In the very short run the conditions of a part of the people can be improved by expropriating entrepreneurs and capitalists and by distributing the booty. But such predatory inroads, which even the *Communist Manifesto* described as "despotic" and as "economically insufficient and untenable," sabotage the operation of the market economy, impair very soon the conditions of all the people and frustrate the endeavors of entrepreneurs and capitalists to make the masses more prosperous. What is good for a quickly vanishing instant, (i.e., in the shortest run) may very soon (i.e., in the long run) result in most detrimental consequences.

Historians are mistaken in explaining the rise of Nazism by referring to real or imaginary adversities and hardships of the German people. What made the Germans support almost unanimously the twenty-five points of the "unalterable" Hitler program was not some conditions which they deemed unsatisfactory, but their expectation that the execution of this program would remove their complaints and render them happier. They turned to Nazism because they lacked common sense and intelligence. They were not judicious enough to recognize in time the disasters that Nazism was bound to bring upon them.

The immense majority of the world's population is extremely poor when compared with the average standard of living of the capitalist nations. But this poverty does not explain their propensity to adopt the communist program. They are anti-capitalistic because they are blinded by envy, ignorance, and too dull to appreciate correctly the causes of their distress. There is but one means to improve their material conditions, namely, to convince them that only capitalism can render them more prosperous.

The worst method to fight communism is that of the Marshall Plan. It gives to the recipients the impression that the United States alone is interested in the preservation of the profit system while their own concerns require a communist regime. The United States, they think, is aiding them because its people have a bad conscience. They themselves pocket this bribe but their sympathies go to the socialist system. The American subsidies make it possible for their governments to conceal partially the disastrous effects of the various socialist measures they have adopted.

Not poverty is the source of socialism, but spurious ideological prepossessions. Most of our contemporaries reject beforehand, without having ever studied them, all the teachings of economics as aprioristic nonsense. Only experience, they maintain, is to be relied upon. But is there any experience that would speak in favor of socialism?

Retorts the socialist: But capitalism creates poverty; look at India and China. The objection is vain. Neither

India nor China has ever established capitalism. Their poverty is the result of the absence of capitalism.

What happened in these and other underdeveloped countries was that they were benefited from abroad by some of the fruits of capitalism without having adopted the capitalist mode of production. European, and in more recent years also American, capitalists invested capital in their areas and thereby increased the marginal productivity of labor and wage rates. At the same time these peoples received from abroad the means to fight contagious diseases, medications developed in the capitalist countries. Consequently mortality rates, especially infant mortality, dropped considerably. In the capitalist countries this prolongation of the average length of life was partially compensated by a drop in the birth rate. As capital accumulation increased more quickly than population, the per head quota of capital invested grew continuously. The result was progressing prosperity. It was different in the countries which enjoyed some of the effects of capitalism without turning to capitalism. There the birth rate did not decline at all or not to the extent required to make the per head quota of capital invested rise. These nations prevent by their policies both the importation of foreign capital and the accumulation of domestic capital. The joint effect of the high birth rate and the absence of an increase in capital is, of course, increasing poverty.

There is but one means to improve the material well-being of men, viz., to accelerate the increase in capital accumulated as against population. No psychological lucubrations, however sophisticated, can alter this fact. There is no excuse whatever for the pursuit of policies which not only fail to attain the ends sought, but even seriously impair conditions.

6. The Moral Condemnation of the Profit Motive

As soon as the problem of profits is raised, people shift it from the praxeological sphere into the sphere of ethical judgments of value. Then everybody glories in the aureole of a saint and an ascetic. He himself does not care for money and material well-being. He serves his fellow men to the best of his abilities unselfishly. He strives after higher and nobler things than wealth. Thank God, he is not one of those egoistic profiteers.

The businessmen are blamed because the only thing they have in mind is to succeed. Yet everybody—without any exception—in acting aims at the attainment of a definite end. The only alternative to success is failure; nobody ever wants to fail. It is the very essence of human nature that man consciously aims at substituting a more satisfactory state of affairs for a less satisfactory. What distinguishes the decent man from the crook is the different goals they are aiming at and the different means they are resorting to in order to attain the ends chosen. But they both want to succeed in their sense. It is logically impermissible to distinguish between people who aim at success and those who do not.

Practically everybody aims at improving the material conditions of his existence. Public opinion takes no offense at the endeavors of farmers, workers, clerks, teachers, doctors, ministers, and people from many other callings to earn as much as they can. But it censures the capitalists and entrepreneurs for their greed.

While enjoying without any scruples all the goods business delivers, the consumer sharply condemns the selfishness of the purveyors of this merchandise. He does not realize that he himself creates their profits by scrambling for the things they have to sell.

Neither does the average man comprehend that profits are indispensable in order to direct the activities of business into those channels in which they serve him best. He looks upon profits as if their only function were to enable the recipients to consume more than he himself does. He fails to realize that their main function is to convey control of the factors of production into the hands of those who best utilize them for his own purposes. He did not, as he thinks, renounce becoming an entrepreneur out of moral scruples. He chose a position with a more modest yield because he lacked the abilities required for entrepreneurship or, in rare cases indeed, because his inclinations prompted him to enter upon another career.

Mankind ought to be grateful to those exceptional men who out of scientific zeal, humanitarian enthusiasm, or religious faith sacrificed their lives, health, and wealth, in the service of their fellow men. But the philistines practice self-deception in comparing themselves with the pioneers of medical X-ray application or with nuns who attend people afflicted with the plague. It is not self-denial that makes the average physician choose a medical career, but the expectation of attaining a respected social position and a suitable income.

Everybody is eager to charge for his services and accomplishments as much as the traffic can bear. In this regard there is no difference between the workers, whether unionized or not, the ministers, and teachers on the one hand and the entrepreneurs on the other hand. None of them has the right to talk as if he were Francis d'Assisi.

There is no other standard of what is morally good and morally bad than the effects produced by conduct upon social cooperation. A—hypothetical—isolated and self-sufficient individual would not in acting have to take into account anything else than his own well-being. Social man must in all his actions avoid indulging in any conduct that would jeopardize the smooth working of the system of social cooperation. In complying with the moral law, man does not sacrifice his own concerns to those of a mythical higher entity, whether it is called class, state, nation, race, or humanity. He curbs some of his own instinctive urges, appetites and greed, that is his short-run concerns, in order to serve best his own—rightly understood or long-run—interests. He forgoes a small gain that he could reap instantly lest he miss a greater but later satisfaction. For the attainment of all human ends, whatever they may be, is conditioned by the preservation and further development of social bonds and interhuman cooperation. What is an indispensable means to intensify social cooperation and to make it possible for more people to survive and to enjoy a higher standard of living is morally good and socially desirable. Those who reject this principle as unchristian ought to ponder over the text: "That thy days may be long upon the land which the Lord thy God giveth thee." They can certainly not deny that capitalism has made man's days longer than they were in the precapitalistic ages.

There is no reason why capitalists and entrepreneurs should be ashamed of earning profits. It is silly that some people try to defend American capitalism by declaring: "The record of American business is good; profits are not too high." The function of entrepreneurs is to make profits; high profits are the proof that they have well performed their task of removing maladjustments of production.

Of course, as a rule capitalists and entrepreneurs are not saints excelling in the virtue of self-denial. But neither are their critics saintly. And with all the regard due to the sublime self-effacement of saints, we cannot help stating the fact that the world would be in a rather desolate condition if it were peopled exclusively by men not interested in the pursuit of material well-being.

7. The Static Mentality

The average man lacks the imagination to realize that the conditions of life and action are in a continual flux. As he sees it, there is no change in the external objects that constitute his well-being. His world view is static and stationary. It mirrors a stagnating environment. He knows neither that the past differed from the present nor that there prevails uncertainty about future things. He is at a complete loss to conceive the function of entrepreneurship because he is unaware of this uncertainty. Like children who take all the things the parents give them without asking any questions, he takes all the goods business offers him. He is unaware of the efforts that supply him with all he needs. He ignores the role of capital accumulation and of entrepreneurial decisions. He simply takes it for granted that a magic table appears at a moment's notice laden with all he wants to enjoy.

This mentality is reflected in the popular idea of socialization. Once the parasitic capitalists and entrepreneurs are thrown out, he himself will get all that they used to consume. It is but the minor error of this expectation that it grotesquely overrates the increment in income, if any, each individual could receive from such a distribution. Much more serious is the fact that it assumes that the only thing required is to continue in the various plants production of those goods they are producing at the moment of the socialization in the ways they were hitherto produced. No account is taken of the necessity to adjust production daily anew to perpetually changing conditions. The dilettante-socialist does not comprehend that a socialization effected fifty years ago would not have socialized the structure of business as it exists today but a very different structure. He does not give a thought to the enormous effort that is needed in order to transform business again and again to render the best possible service.

This dilettantish inability to comprehend the essential issues of the conduct of production affairs is not only manifested in the writings of Marx and Engels. It permeates no less the contributions of contemporary psuedo-economics.

The imaginary construction of an evenly rotating economy is an indispensable mental tool of economic thinking. In order to conceive the function of profit and loss, the economist constructs the image of a hypothetical, although unrealizable, state of affairs in which nothing changes, in which tomorrow does not differ at all from today and in which consequently no maladjustments can arise and no need for any alteration in the conduct of business emerges. In the frame of this imaginary construction there are no entrepreneurs and no entrepreneurial profits and losses. The wheels turn spontaneously as it were. But the real world in which men live and have to work can never duplicate the hypothetical world of this mental makeshift.

Now one of the main shortcomings of the mathematical economists is that they deal with this evenly rotating economy—they call it the static state—as if it were something really existing. Prepossessed by the fallacy that economics is to be treated with mathematical methods, they concentrate their efforts upon the analysis of static states which, of course, allow a description in sets of simultaneous differential equations. But this mathematical treatment virtually avoids any reference to the real problems of economics. It indulges in quite useless mathematical play without adding anything to the comprehension of the problems of human acting and producing. It creates the misunderstanding as if the analysis of static states were the main concern of economics. It confuses a merely ancillary tool of thinking with reality.

The mathematical economist is so blinded by his epistemological prejudice that he simply fails to see what the tasks of economics are. He is anxious to show us that socialism is realizable under static conditions. As static conditions, as he himself admits, are unrealizable, this amounts merely to the assertion that in an unrealizable state of the world socialism would be realizable. A very valuable result, indeed, of a hundred years of the joint work of hundreds of authors, taught at all universities, publicized in innumerable textbooks and monographs and in scores of allegedly scientific magazines!

There is no such thing as a static economy. All the conclusions derived from preoccupation with the image of static states and static equilibrium are of no avail for the description of the world as it is and will always be.

C. The Alternative

A social order based on private control of the means of production cannot work without entrepreneurial action and entrepreneurial profit and, of course, entrepreneurial loss. The elimination of profit, whatever methods may be resorted to for its execution, must transform society into a senseless jumble. It would create poverty for all.

In a socialist system there are neither entrepreneurs nor entrepreneurial profit and loss. The supreme director of the socialist commonwealth would, however, have to strive in the same way after a surplus of proceeds over costs as the entrepreneurs do under capitalism. It is not the task of this essay to deal with socialism. Therefore it is not necessary to stress the point that, not being able to apply any kind of economic calculation, the socialist chief would never know what the costs and what the proceeds of his operations are.

What matters in this context is merely the fact that there is no third system feasible. There cannot be any such thing as a non-socialist system without entrepreneurial profit and loss. The endeavors to eliminate profits from the capitalist system are merely destructive. They disintegrate capitalism without putting anything in its place. It is this that we have in mind in maintaining that they result in chaos.

Men must choose between capitalism and socialism. They cannot avoid this dilemma by resorting to a capitalist system without entrepreneurial profit. Every step toward the elimination of profit is progress on the way toward social disintegration.

In choosing between capitalism and socialism people are implicitly also choosing between all the social institutions which are the necessary accompaniment of each of these systems, its "superstructure" as Marx said. If control of production is shifted from the hands of entrepreneurs, daily anew elected by a plebiscite of the consumers, into the hands of the supreme commander of the "industrial armies" (Marx and Engels) or of the "armed workers" (Lenin), neither representative government nor any civil liberties can survive. Wall Street, against which the self-styled idealists are battling, is merely a symbol. But the walls of the Soviet prisons within which all dissenters disappear forever are a hard fact.